Spiffy

Angie's Patterns - Volume 5

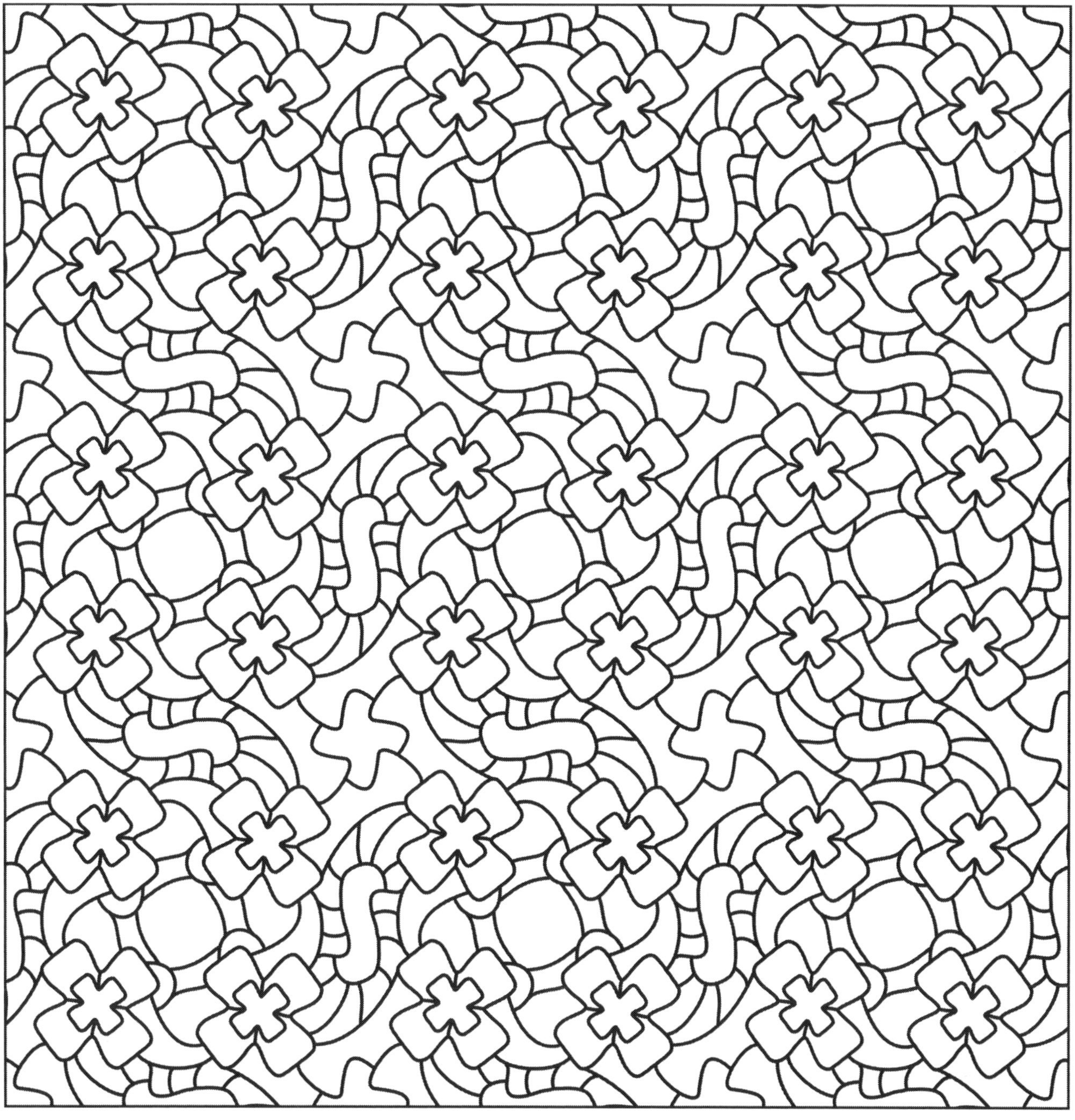

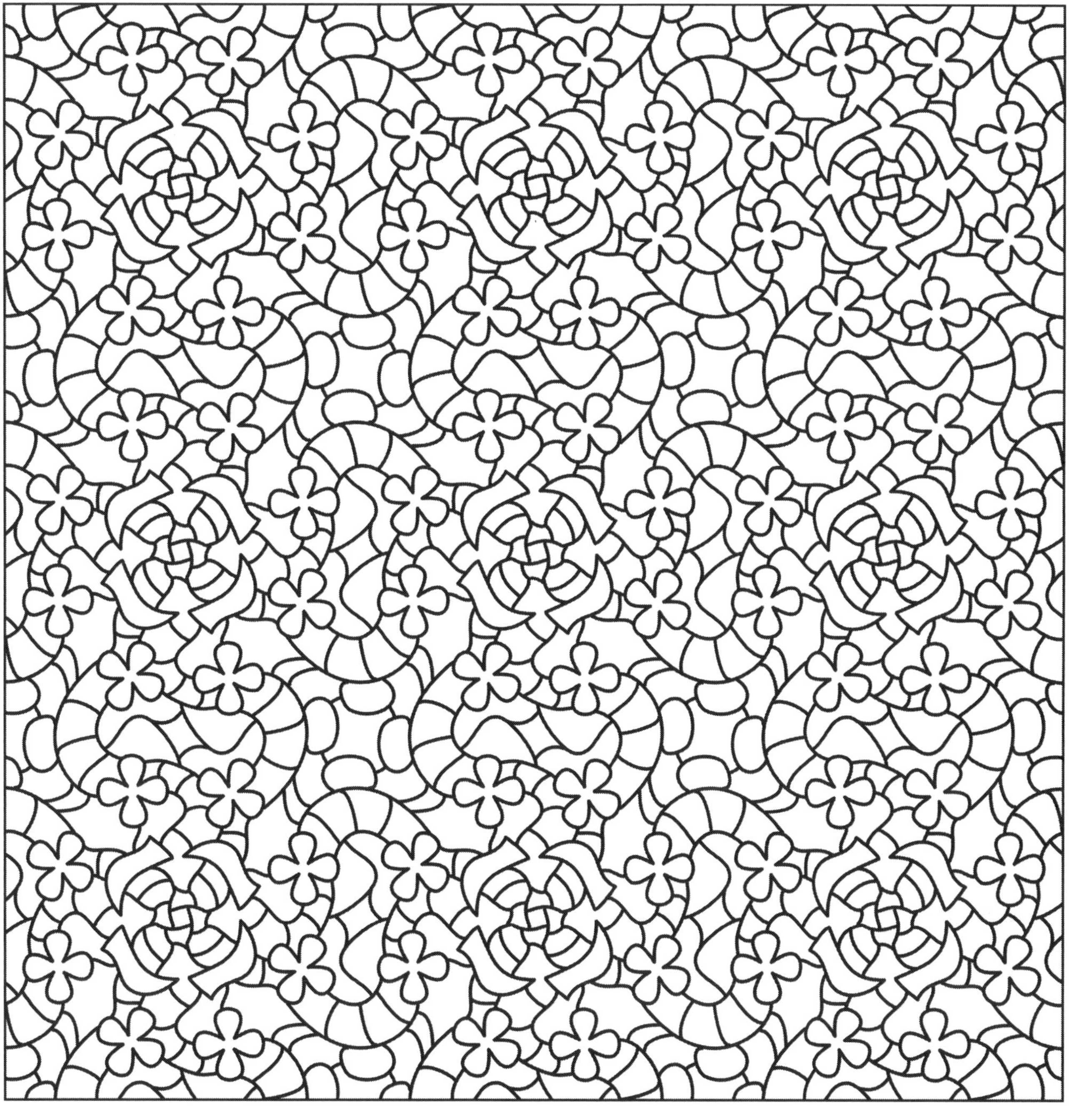

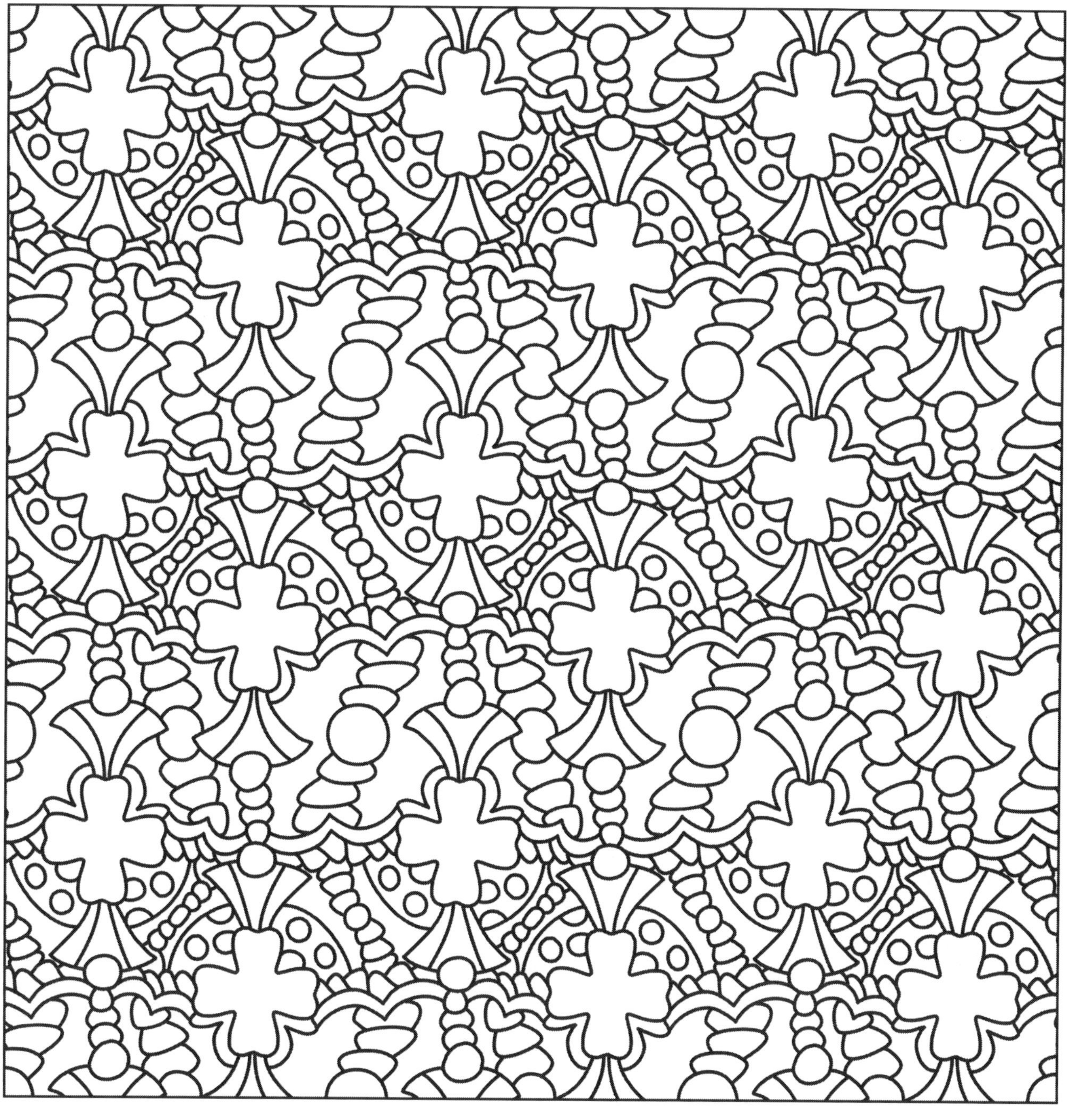

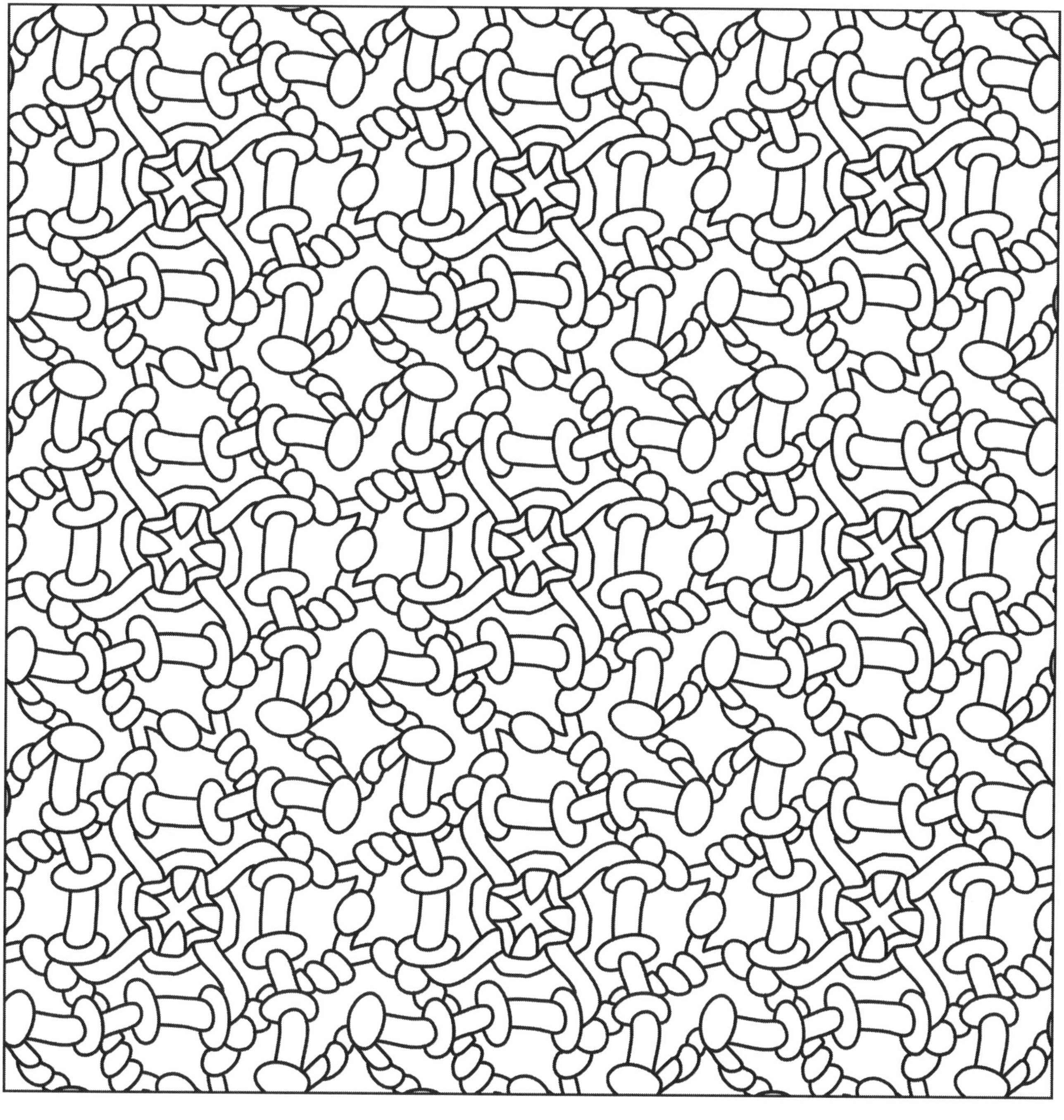

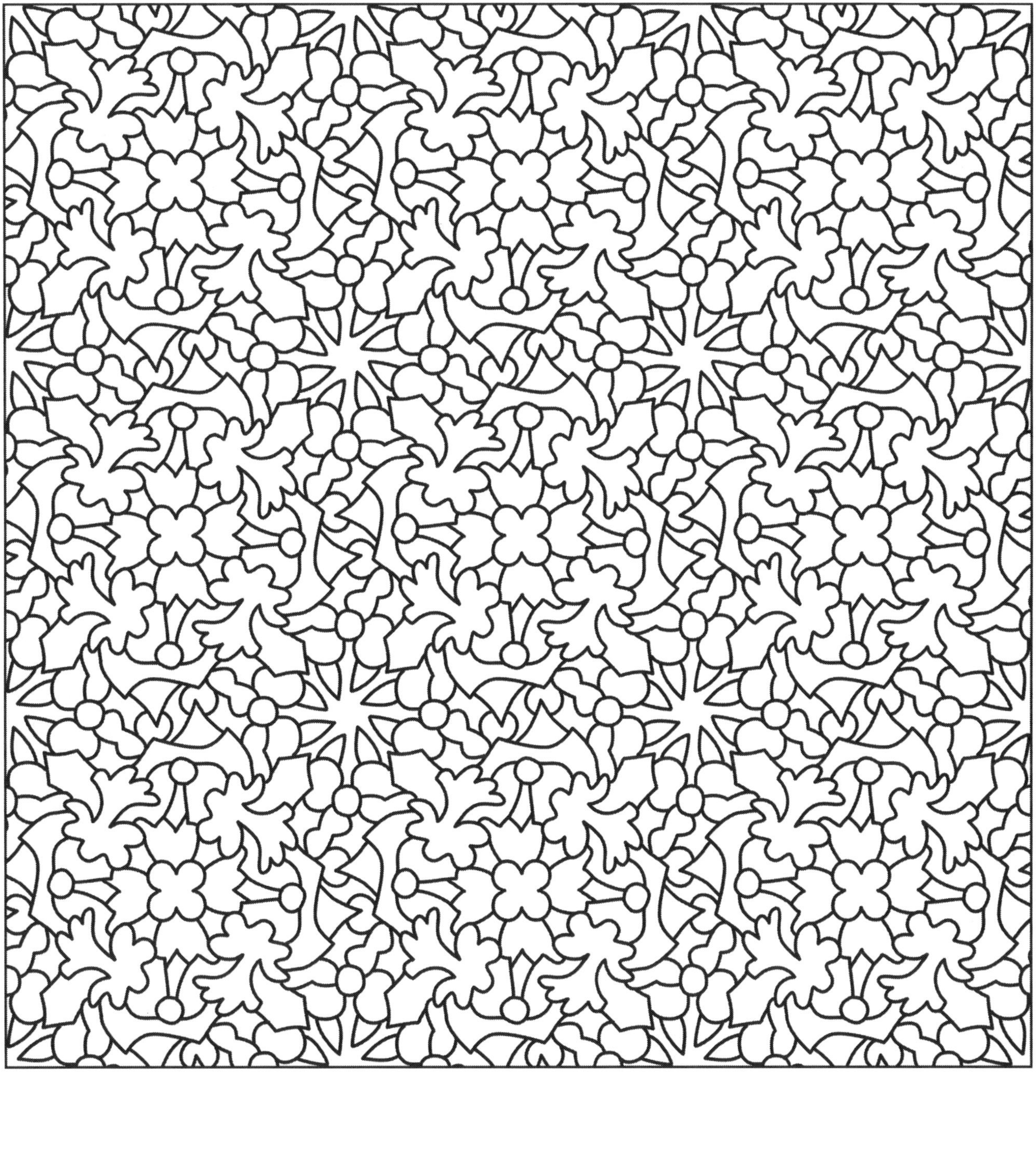

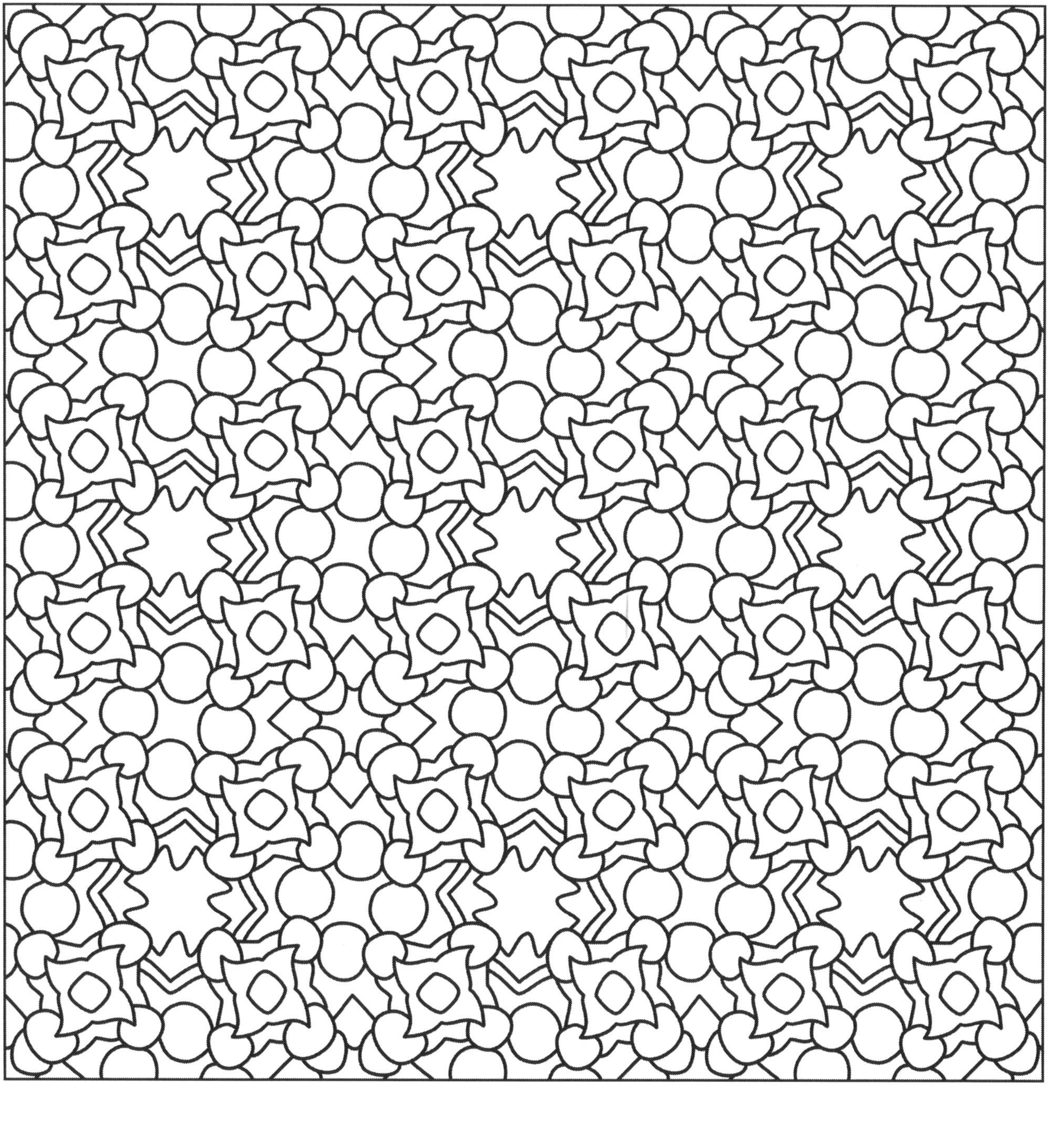

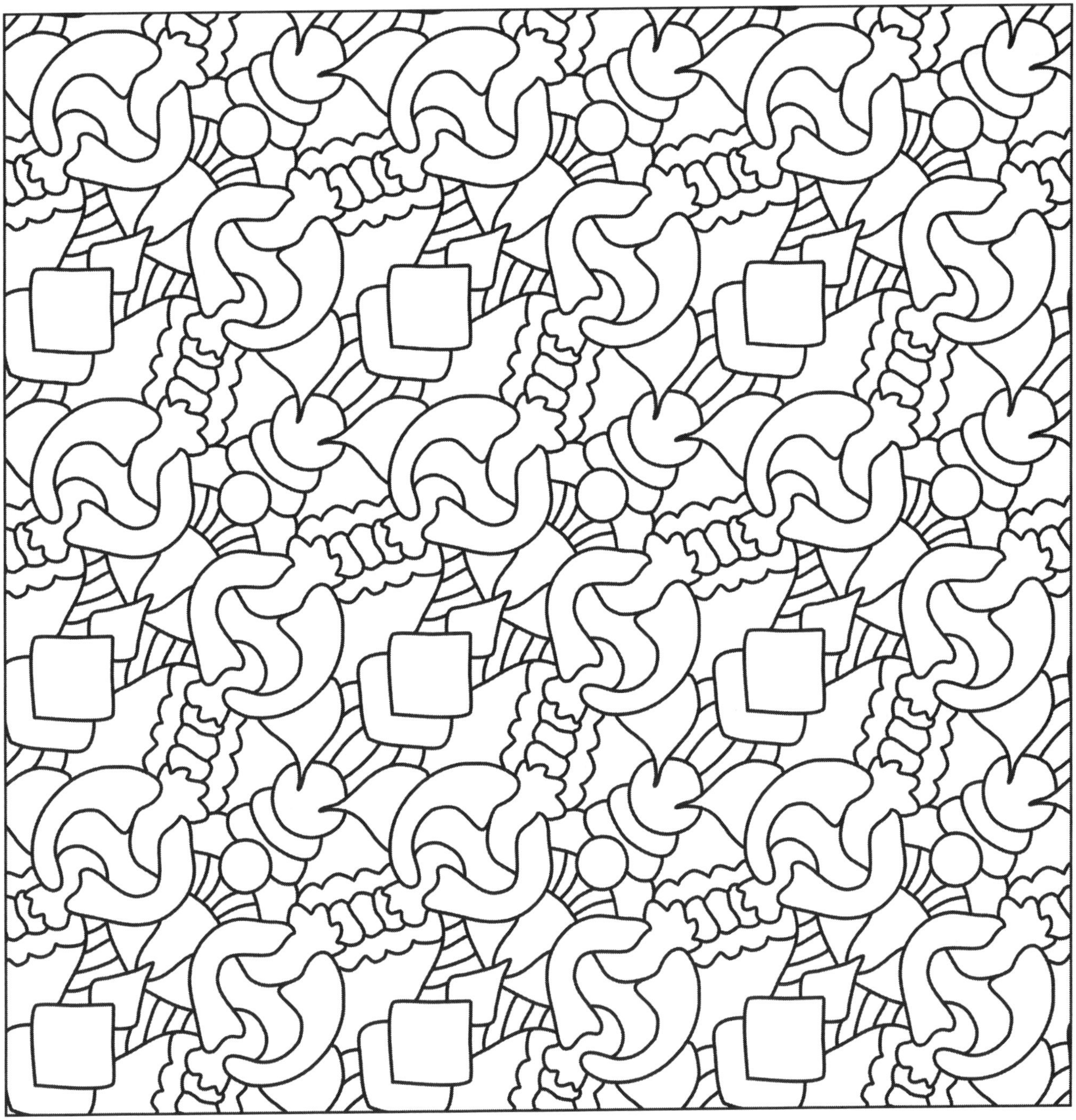

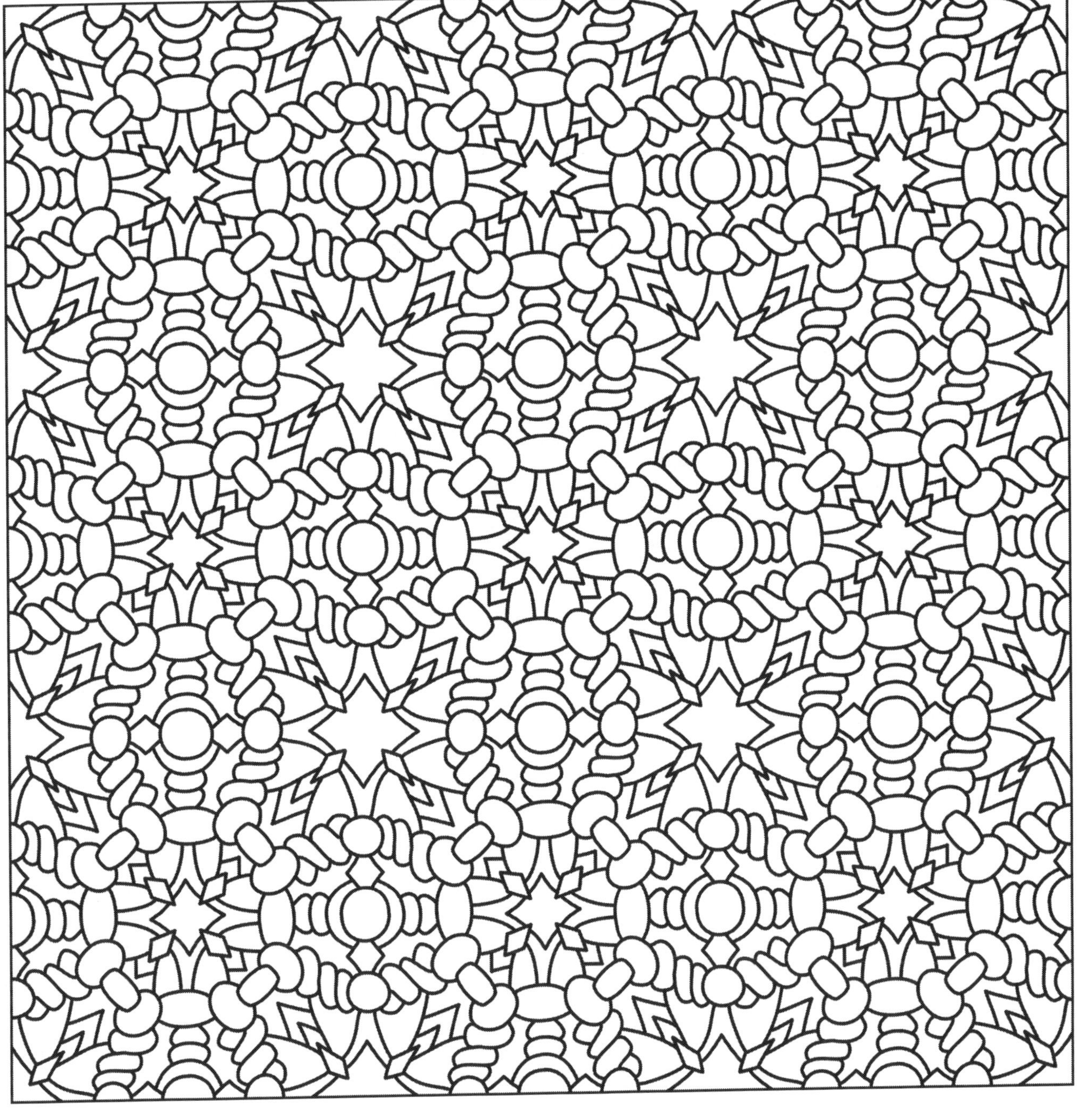

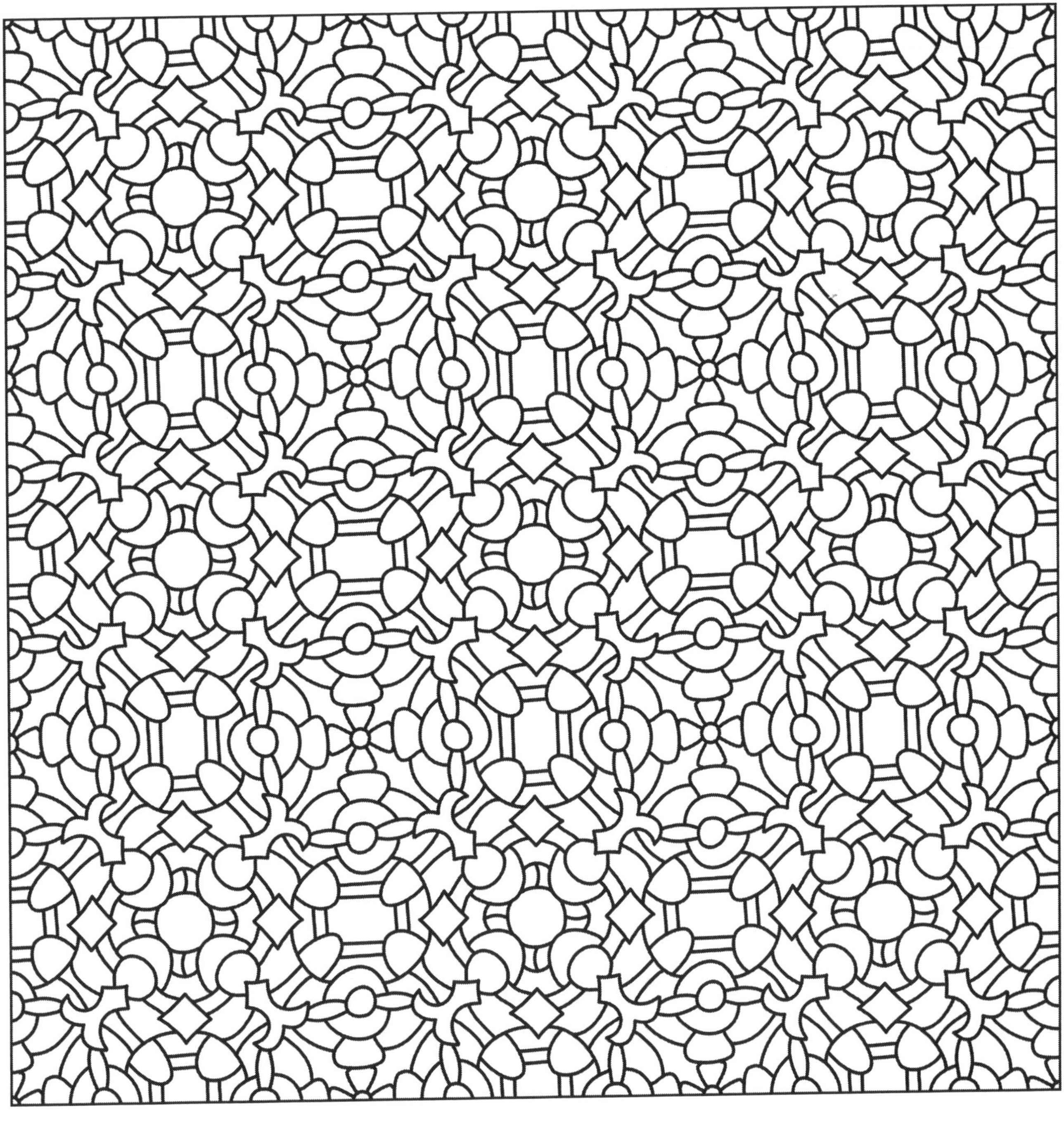

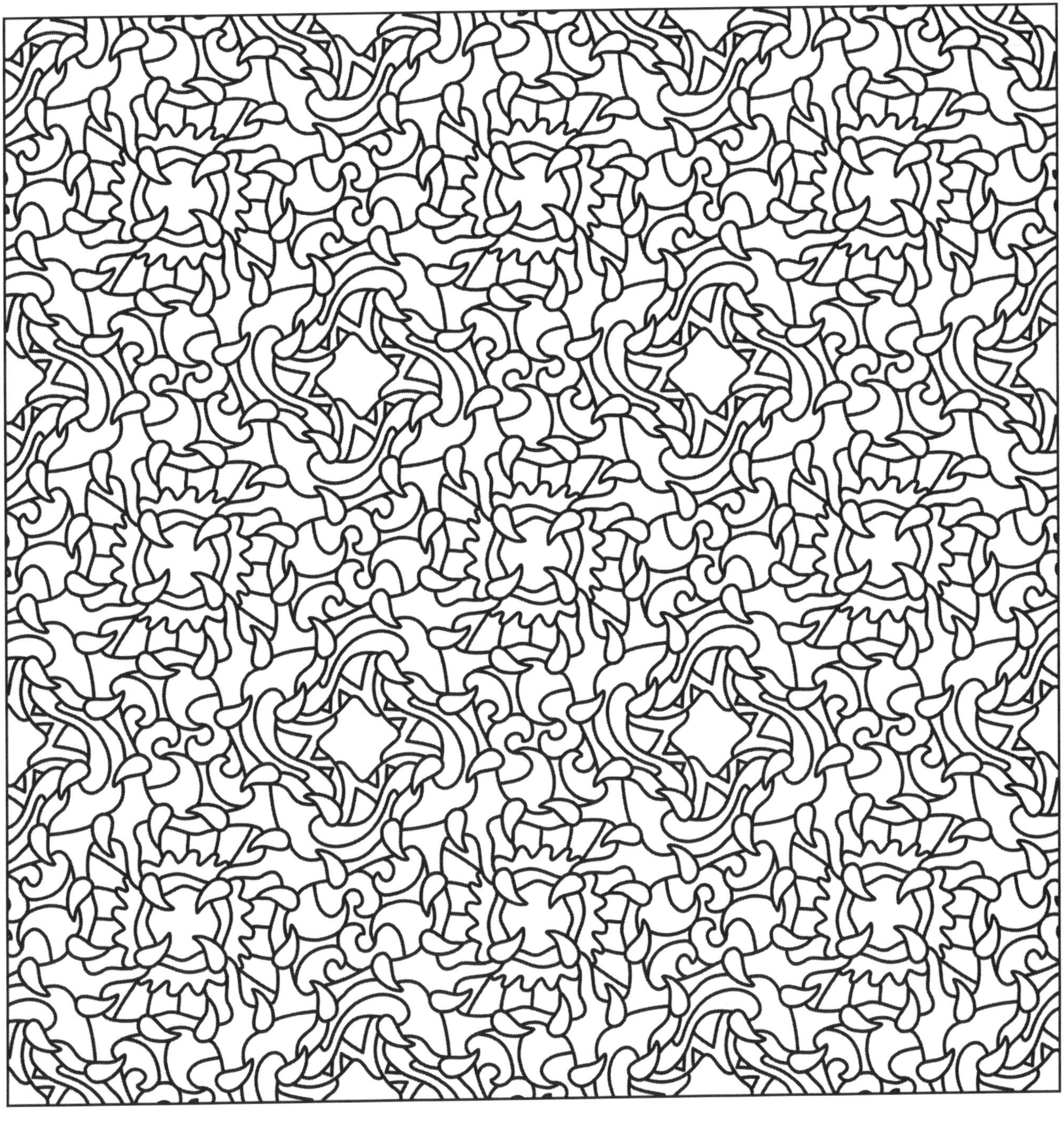

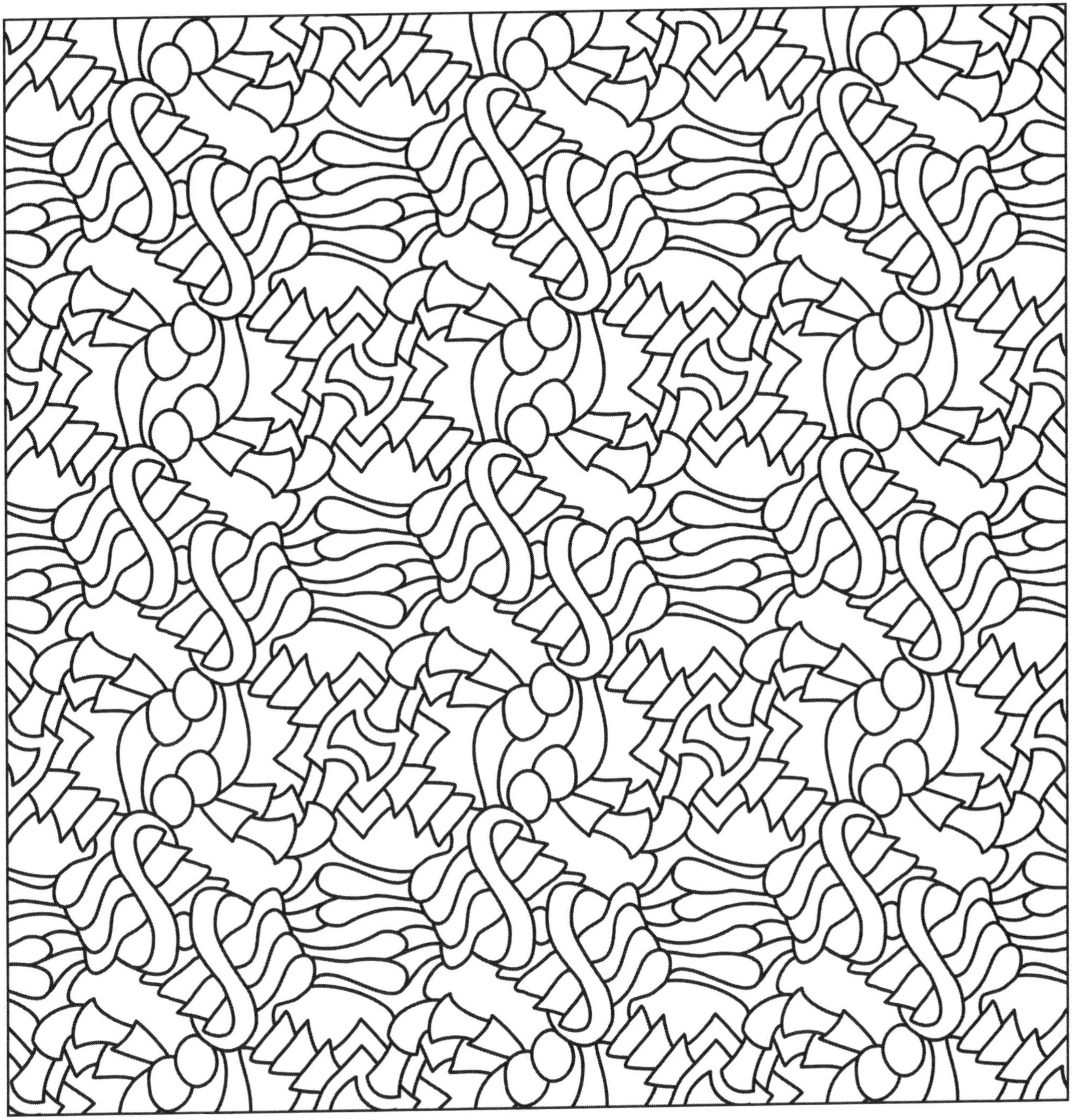

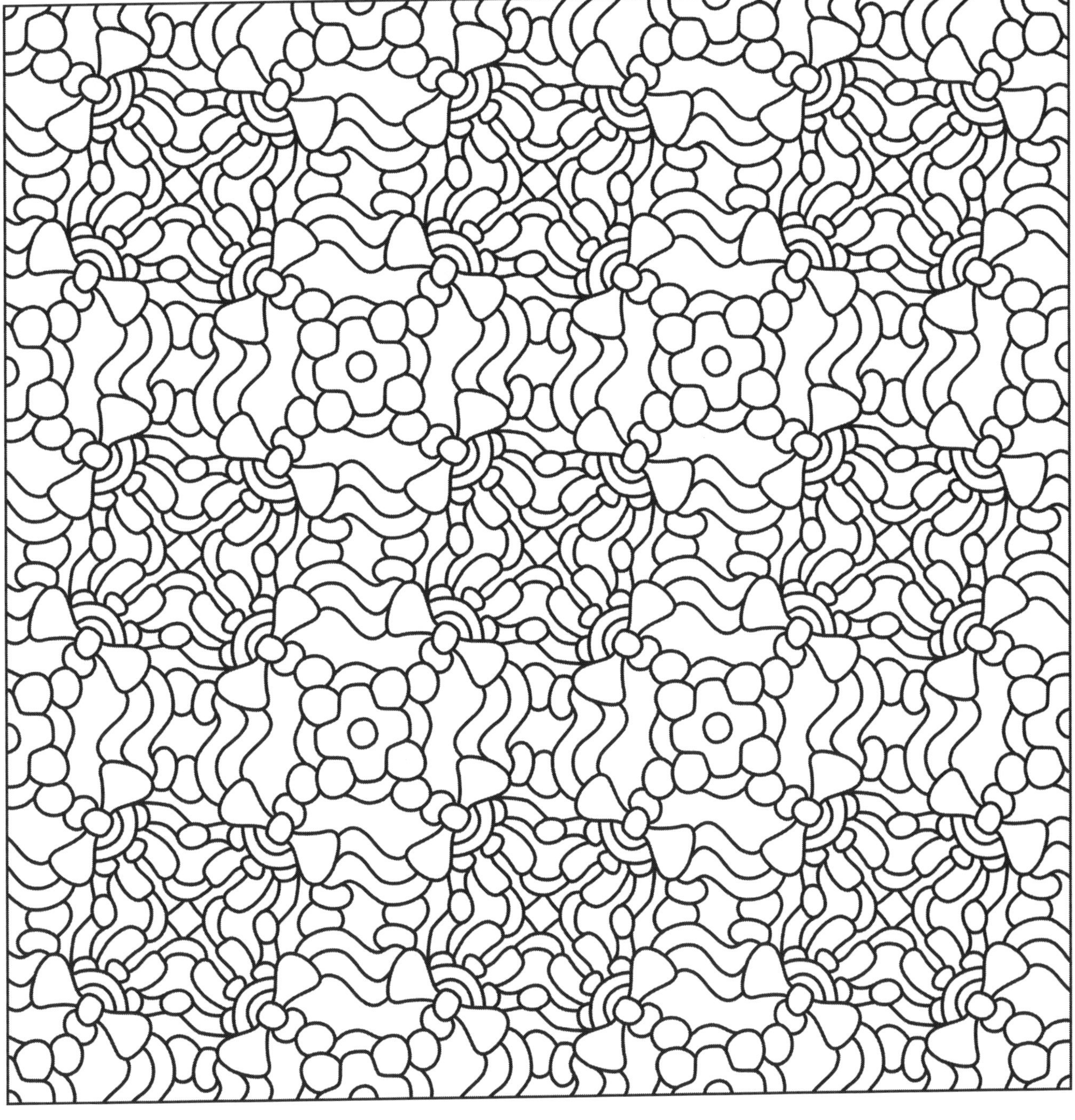

Visit Angie's website
for special web exclusives for colorists.

www.AngieGrace.com

31546641R00059

Made in the USA
Lexington, KY
21 February 2019